Dane Love is the author of numerous books on Scotland in general and on Ayrshire in particular. He was born in Cumnock but now lives in the countryside near Auchinleck. He is descended from Robin Love, who fought for Bonnie Prince Charlie at the battles of Prestonpans and Culloden. A member of Ayrshire Archaeological and Natural History Society, he is also the Honorary Secretary of the Scottish Covenanter Memorials Association and a Fellow of the Society of Antiquaries of Scotland. He works as a Principal Teacher at Irvine Royal Academy. In his free time, he enjoys travelling around Scotland with his wife and two children, visiting historic sites and doing research.

Tolbooth, Parish Church and Irvine Bridge.

Title Page and Back Cover: Ordnance Survey Six Inch Map of Irvine in 1856
Following Page: John Woodside, who delivered for Robert Downie, butcher, 127-129 High Street.

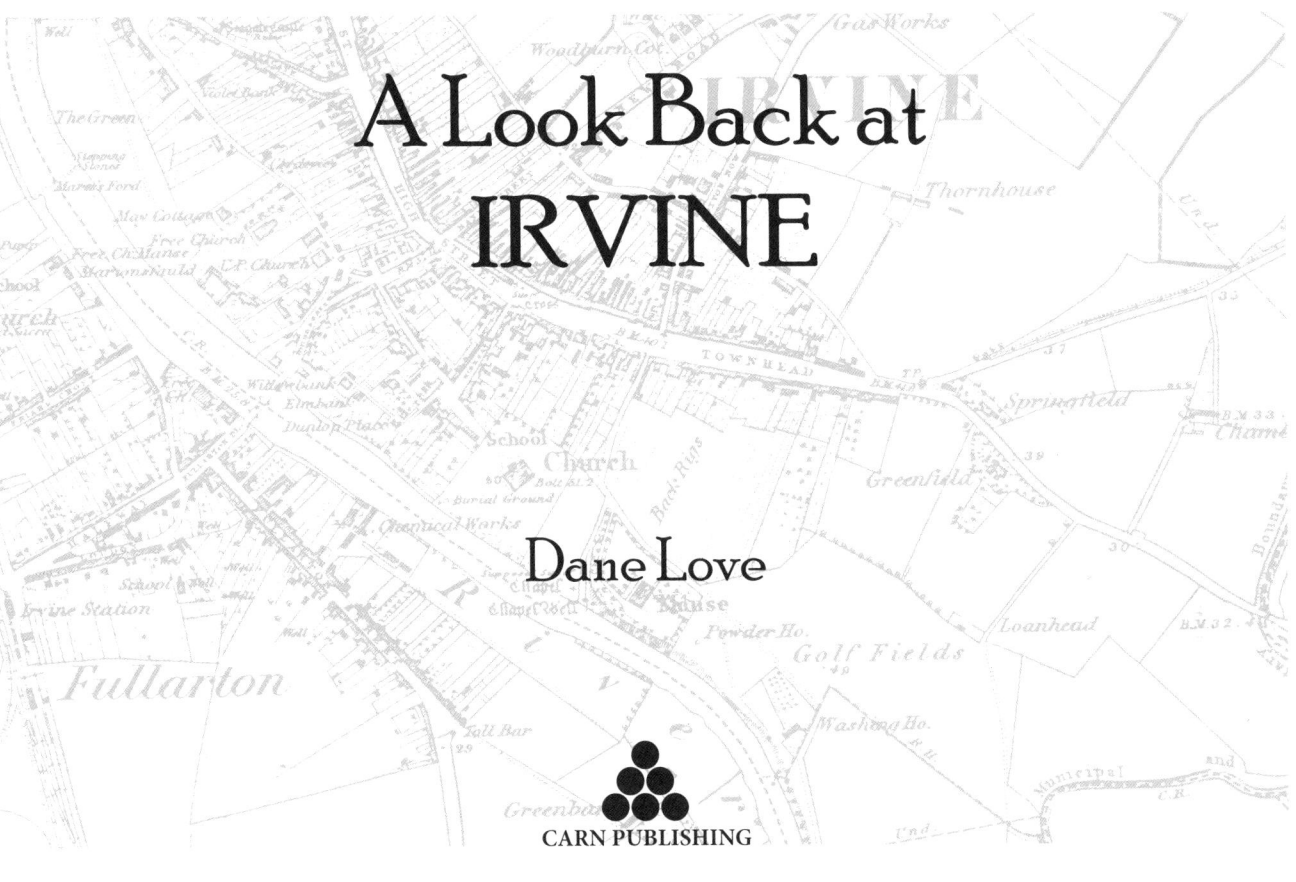

A Look Back at IRVINE

Dane Love

CARN PUBLISHING

© Dane Love, 2019.
First Published in Great Britain, 2019.

ISBN - 978 1 911043 07 2

Published by Carn Publishing Ltd.,
Lochnoran House,
Auchinleck,
Ayrshire, KA18 3JW.

www.carnpublishing.com

Printed by Bell & Bain Ltd.,
Glasgow, G46 7UQ.

The right of the author to be identified as the author of this work has been asserted by him in accordance with the Copyright, Designs and Patents Act, 1988.

All rights reserved. No part of this publication can be reproduced, stored, or transmitted in any form, or by any means, electronic, mechanical or photocopying, recording or otherwise, without the express written permission of the publisher.

Introduction

Irvine is a town unique in Scotland, being the only New Town built around an ancient town. The origins of the burgh appear to be timeless, and some claim that this was the original Roman port of Vindogara, but there has been little Roman evidence coming to light, apart from some Roman coins found in the High Street. In 1140 David I created the town a burgh, under Hugh de Morville, with jurisdiction over Cunninghame. Irvine Castle was constructed, perhaps near to the present Seagate Castle. A parish was created, extending inland for four miles, but squashed between that of Kilwinning and Dundonald. It extends to 4,191 acres. In 1372 the town was raised in status to a Royal Burgh by King Robert II, though earlier dates of 1322 and 1308 have been claimed.

Irvine has been involved in some important events in Scottish history. In 1297 the Treaty of Irvine was signed, when the Scots army (camped at Knadgerhill) capitulated to the English without a fight. In 1412 a monastery of the Carmelite friars was founded in the area, hence Friars' Croft. Mary Queen of Scots visited the town on Sunday 1 August 1563, probably staying at Seagate Castle, guest of Hugh Montgomerie, 3rd Earl of Eglinton. In the late sixteenth century there were a number of cases of witchcraft in the town. In 1666 two Covenanting martyrs were executed at the gallows on Irvine Moor for their part in the Pentland Rising. They were James Blackwood and Andrew MacCall. On 31 December 1823 a tombstone was erected over their grave in the kirkyard. Smuggling was rife for a period, with corn brought from Ireland and whisky from Arran and Argyll.

Originally, Fullarton, or Halfway, was outwith the control of the burgh, being a burgh of barony of its own, located in the parish of Dundonald. From 1690 until 1823 it was thought to have been united with Irvine, but in the latter year it was discovered that this was not the case. However, in 1881 it was added to the burgh by an act of extension.

The harbour became a considerable influence in the

development of the town, and the old port at the foot of the Seagate was replaced with the present harbour. Over the centuries it appears to have waxed and waned in trade, vying with Ayr to be the largest port in the county. Hides, coal, chrome ore, fireclay products and other goods were exported, in 1760 the port being the third largest in Scotland. Imports were timber, linen cloth and limestone. Irvine Harbour Trust controlled the port until 1912, after which it was taken over by a shipbuilder and subsequently ICI.

The harbour was often used for the export of coal, much of which was mined within the parish. One of the earliest coal works was established in 1686, when miners were plied with ten pints of ale and two cakes of bread when coal was discovered. Coal mines existed at Annicklodge, Bartonholm, Bogside, Broomlands, Eglinton and Sourlie. Mining communities were created at most of these locations. The last coal dug in the parish was by opencast means.

The arrival of the railway in 1839 increased trade, with the Glasgow, Paisley, Kilmarnock & Ayr Railway opening a station at Montgomery Street. A branch was laid to the harbour in 1847. The Lanarkshire & Ayrshire branch of the Caledonian Railway arrived in 1890, adding a second station to the town, located off Bank Street. This was also a period of considerable improvement, running water being introduced in 1878 from a reservoir six miles away at a cost of £40,000.

In the mid twentieth century, Irvine burgh had plans for growth, and in 1959 signed an agreement with Glasgow to take some of the city's population overspill, requiring the building of 1,400 council houses.

Industry flourished for a time, with chemical works being created by William Henderson (1871), the Caledonian Forge of 1891, and Portland Glass Company (1925). John Cowan & Co. Ltd, soap manufacturers, claimed to be one of the oldest firms in Ayrshire. The manufacture of hosiery and woollens was a major employer in the town for many years, the introduction of hand sewing around 1790 being the catalyst. The armaments factory was opened in 1937. Volvo began making trucks in 1975.

In the 1970s and 1980s Irvine went into a manufacturing decline, in 1979 the town having the unenviable reputation of having the highest unemployment rate in Great Britain, at 15.5%, resulting in The Proclaimers referring to 'Irvine no more' in the hit song, 'Letter from America'. For a time, the future of employment appeared to be in electronics and computer manufacture, with a number of businesses opening plants to assemble computers or else make components. Among these businesses were Conner Peripherals, Electroconnect, Prestwick Circuits, Escom, Digital, Fullarton and Itech, all of which have gone.

Leisure has played an important part in Irvine's history, with Bogside race course, established in 1808 by the Earl of Eglinton, being an important steeplechase centre and home of the Scottish Grand National until the course was closed in 1965. Golf courses were established at Ravenspark (1907), Bogside (1887), Glasgow Gailes (1892), Western Gailes (1897) and Southern Gailes, or Dundonald Links (2003). More recently, the Magnum Leisure Centre proved popular.

The promotion of Irvine's heritage has grown slowly over the years, with the Scottish Maritime Museum being centred in the town, with a rebuilt Linthouse building being brought from Govan. The museum also has floating exhibits off pontoons in the harbour, a shipyard workers' flat and shop at the harbour. The Big Idea, a centre celebrating Scottish invention, located across the Bridge of Inventors from the harbour side, on Ardeer peninsula, was short-lived, operating from 2000 until 2003.

Irvine today is a town that is still developing. It is the commercial and political centre for the North Ayrshire Council area, and housing has extended to the north-east, as far as Perceton and Sourlie. The population in the 2011 census was reckoned to be around 34,390.

The Bridgegate

The Bridgegate was probably developed as a street once the bridge was constructed over the River Irvine. The roadway leads from the Cross down to Irvine Bridge, which has been replaced by the Rivergate Shopping Centre since 1976. This view depicts the street looking north-east towards the Cross, with the entrance to West Road leaving to the left, next to the pillar box. Beyond the shop on the left with the sunshades was the Lochlomond or Lomond Vaults pub, and just beyond it was the lane known as the Wee Groop. At the turn of the twentieth century, the pub was owned by J. Hutchison. The three-storey building with the small pediment was the Irvine and Fullarton Literary and Social Institute. This organisation was founded in 1867 by solicitor William D. McJannet, with subscribers contributing towards the cost of buying the former Baptist Church and erecting new premises, built adjoining the former. The architect was John Armour, and the building cost £3,000, but included three shops and two houses which were let. Within were reading and recreation rooms. The opening night comprised of a soiree, and in 1871 Diorama slides were shown. A report in the *Glasgow Herald* of 8 January 1907 details the annual general meeting. At the time Alexander Parker was the president; W. Lamont was treasurer and secretary. The year-ending financial details had a surplus of over £50, the year being the most successful to date. The assets of the institute that year were £2,194 8s 9d. The loan on the property was £1,300, leaving a credit balance of £894 8s 9d. MacJannet was re-elected as Hon. President, Alex Parker as President, and Messrs Johnston and Wark as Vice Presidents. Opposite the institute is the entrance to the Trinity Church, with railings and gates. Prior to the erection of the church, this part of the street was lined with more properties. Only buildings from the cross to the light-coloured gable, adjoining Hill Street, survive, the left-hand side of the picture demolished and replaced by Bridgegate House in 1974, designed originally by David Gosling, but restyled in 2013.

The Bridgegate at foot of Hill Street

The Irvine and Fullarton Literary Institute on the left gave access to the Empire Picture House, and this old photograph shows it with posters advertising children's matinees. The sign reading 'Shipping and Emigration' was on the premises of A. S. MacAllister & Co. This was Globe House, a drapery, but also agent for shipping. MacAllister was a town councillor for a time, as well as being a trustee of Irvine Harbour Company. His wife served on the school board, the first local woman to hold public office. Beyond Globe House, nearer the Cross, was the Buttercup Dairy Company's premises. The buildings on the right mainly survive, but their shop fronts have been altered over the years. The first shop on the right was probably Thomas Dunlop, jewellers, at the time the photograph was taken, then Gaw the jewellers. Next door was Miss Boyd's shop, where she sold books and stationery. William Kerr was next, where he sold tobacco and associated pipes, etc. The lighter coloured building was the bakery operated by Mrs John Crawford – she also had a tearoom inside. Another bakery was a few doors along – originally (in the late 1800s) run by David Maitland (died 1892), followed by his wife, but taken over by their former apprentice, John Short, in 1906. In 1945 the firm was re-established as John Short & Sons. Beyond Shorts were shops occupied by John Clark, tailor, the Wright Brothers, game dealers, and George Gorman, spirit merchant. The latter shop became the Delta Bar. The shop with the large clock hanging outside was occupied for many years by James Gilchrist, watchmaker and jeweller, established in 1835. Next door was the shop belonging to David Wilson, draper and clothier, established in 1867. At the end of the street, just before the Cross, were a couple of shops occupied by shoemakers. At the very corner were the premises of William Higgins & Co., and next to it was William Turnbull's shoe shop – 'English, Swiss and Maybole goods, of the newest and most fashionable styles'. Robert Wilson's shoe shop was across the street next to the Buttercup Dairy.

Bridgegate

Taken from Irvine Bridge, this image shows the bottom end of Bridgegate. The buildings on the right all post-date 1881, the year the council obtained an act which allowed them to order the demolition of their predecessors for road-widening. On the right is the Bridge Hotel. The building was erected in 1885 by William MacBride and in the following year was purchased by Charles S. MacDougall for £1,500. The hotel was later owned by William Lamont, a former Scottish international footballer. He had played for Renton, Queen's Park and Third Lanark. He received his cap in 1885. In March 1938, whilst rising from his bed, he fell into the fireplace and his clothing caught fire, resulting in his death. Prior to the hotel being erected, the author Edgar Allan Poe spent a few months at Bridgegate House, which existed here. He was only six years old, but found Irvine oppressive. On the extreme right of the photograph is a single-storey building, at one time the premises of Yule the glazier. The lane between here and the hotel led to two sizeable villas – Willowbank and Elmbank, now demolished. Elmbank was purchased in 1876 by Mr Holmes, of Holmes & Young, coachbuilders. Willowbank was, in 1900, the home of Mr Gillespie, dentist. On the left side of the photograph is a tin shed, at the time 'To Let', which was part of the former gasworks. Irvine gasworks was established in 1829 by the Irvine Gas Light Company (who had collected subscriptions for the previous two years). In 1908 the business was taken over by the Irvine Gas Company and it continued to produce town gas until 1964. Some of the earliest buildings lit by gas were the parish church (1831), Royal Academy (1832) and the Crown Hotel (1832). The works were moved to larger premises at Bank Street, in the gusset between it and Cotton Row. The tall buildings to the left, behind the lamp standard, form what was known as Rattan (or Rotten) Row. Within one of the buildings was a branch of the British Linen Bank, at 30 Bridgegate.

Waterside

Waterside Street was originally a street of two contrasts – the denser line of houses at the south end, near to Fullarton Place, and the salubrious semi-villas and villas beyond Friars' Croft Street. The houses built along the edge of the River Irvine, seen in this old postcard, date from the early part of the nineteenth century. Many of them were built by notable merchants and businessmen, moving to a more upmarket part of the town. The only downside was their susceptibility to flooding. In the picture there is no fence separating the road and the river, which often resulted in problems. For example, in August 1851 a young boy of around five years, surnamed Brown, had his bonnet blown off and into the river. He tried to reclaim it, but he fell into the water and was swept away by the flow, and drowned. His body was found a couple of hours later caught on a paling near to Queen's Bridge. The first house on the left of the picture was Marine Lodge, with its flagstaff in the garden, occupied around 1900 by Robert F. Longmuir, ship broker and county councillor. Next door was Marionsfauld, at one time the home of Lt Col William Shaw, followed by the Fullarton Free Church Manse. Just beyond Marress Street was the Fullarton Parish Church Manse. The houses beyond were erected sporadically from 1856 until 1908, the last terrace of three seen in the photograph being erected between 1895 and 1908. Two of the houses were occupied by captains, J. MacMillan and Henry Abram. A number of doctors have also made their home in this street, including Dr W. A. Paterson. At the bend in the river was the Maress Ford, where stepping stones once crossed the river to the Low Green. Back towards Montgomery Street was a large house known as Bower Lodge, at one time the home of George Robertson (1758-1832), who wrote a number of historical books on Ayrshire, including the notable *Topographical Description of Ayrshire* and *Rural Recollections*. The house was sold in 1873 by Mr Bone to Boyle Lindsay for £650.

High Street

Photographed from near the Cross, looking south-east up the High Street, this picture dates from the turn of the twentieth century. On the left is the 'Irvine Ironmongery Warehouse'. This was demolished and replaced with a supermarket, for a time operated by Somerfield. It was later the co-operative's supermarket. At the corner of High Street and Bank Street was Irvine and Fullarton Co-operative Society's principal shop in the town. This had been erected in 1932 to plans by W. F. Valentine and within it was the Caledonian Hall, named to commemorate the Caledonian Inn which stood there beforehand. On the ground floor, to the right of the ornamental arched doorway, was a shop occupied by A. Cuthbert & Son. It was taken over by William G. Williamson, who sold butcher meat for many years. The next shop was occupied at the time of the picture by J. Mitchell. He succeeded A. B. Stewart, spirit merchant. This building was also known as the Wheatsheaf Inn, replacing the older inn of that name which stood on roughly the same site. (This corner of the cross was redeveloped and the street frontage was moved back a few yards.) The following shop was the Horse Bar, then James Cruickshanks' fish and chip shop. In the 1935 directory he is listed as a 'restaurateur'. Today it is Mamma's fish and chip shop, owned by the Pellegrini family. Next to the Town House was the Whip Inn, at the time of the photograph owned by James Agnew. It was taken over by Alexander Cook. The building was demolished after the Second World War. In front of the Town House was the site of the market cross of the burgh, originally located at the south-east end of the old tolbooth. In 1694 the market cross was destroyed when the council decided to build a new Meal Market adjoining. Visible in the photograph is the statue of Rt. Hon. David Boyle of Shewalton, Lord Justice Clerk (1772-1853). It was erected by public subscription in 1867 and sculpted by John Steell. It was removed to Castle Street in 1929.

Fullarton Place

Looking back across Irvine Bridge towards the town centre, dominated by the spire of Irvine United Presbyterian Church (latterly Trinity Church), this old image depicts Fullarton Place. A short street, it links Montgomery Street with the bridge. On the left is the start of Waterside Street, the other side of the crossroads being Loudon Street. Half way along the street on the right is the end of Fullarton Street. This part of Irvine is really the separate community of Fullarton, for once the River Irvine is crossed from the town centre, one enters the parish of Dundonald. This parish difference caused some difficulty for the royal burgh over the years, especially as the harbour was beyond their jurisdiction. Eventually, the extended burgh of Irvine was able to have some control of harbour matters.

On the left of the picture is the Bute and Ayr Arms Inn, a popular hostelry in this part of the town. At the turn of the century it was run by Miss M. J. Crawford. The last owner was Willie Kilmarnock, who was noted as a football player, especially with Motherwell Football Club, which he captained when they won the Scottish Cup in 1952. On his retiral from football, Kilmarnock returned to Irvine, where he had been born in the High Street, and purchased this inn and a sports shop.

Not visible, at the end of the street on the left, was the Fullarton Hotel, at the bridge-end. Behind it were stables and ostlery services. Adjacent to it was the access drive to Fullarton Free Church, opened on 2 November 1873.

At the end of the street to the right is the Victoria Buildings, a block of five shops. That next to the bridge was occupied by Henry Downs, carpenter. Next door was John Hall's shop – he sold hardware, books and stationery. Following was Alexander Wyllie, then Miss Crawford's grocery. The final shop was a drapery, run by Robert Goodfellow. Fullarton Street strikes to the right, on this side of the billboards. In the large sandstone building to the right was James MacCrossan's offices. He was an insurance agent.

Fullarton Place

This photograph was taken around 1970, looking south-west along Fullarton Place towards Montgomery Street. The shop on the right was Sadie's boutique, where women's fashions and lingerie were sold. Sadie apparently worked for another shopkeeper, but her window-dressing skill was noticed, and it was suggested to her that she opened her own shop, which took place in the 1960s. At one time there were two shops under the name Sadie – the other was in Bridgegate. When the two areas of the town were redeveloped, a new shop was opened in Bank Street, where Sadie's daughter, Margaret Murphy, continued to run it until 2015. Next again, at the corner with Waterside, was the Bute and Ayr Arms. The left-hand part of the inn was at one time a small sweetie shop. Beyond Waterside junction, where the lollypop man is standing, Montgomery Street stretches into the distance, passing below the station bridge, and continuing as far as the sawmill of Andrew Wright and Nephew. Historically, this street was known as Halfway, believed to derive from the words 'haaf way', meaning the road to the sea. The street was renamed in 1882 in honour of the poet, James Montgomery (1771-1854), who was born on the south side of the street, the cottage at number 26 long bearing a stone plaque in his honour. This is now located in Fullarton Parish Church. His father, Rev John Montgomery, set up a congregation of the Moravian Church in Braid Close, off Halfway, in 1771, but this did not survive very long. Montgomery was noted as a writer of hymns, some of which still appear in modern hymn books. He worked as a journalist, editing the *Sheffield Iris*, but his views sometimes resulted in his imprisonment. His poetry was successful, especially *The Wanderer of Switzerland*, published in 1802. He campaigned against the slave trade, using his talents to produce *The West Indies*, and against the use of young boys as chimney sweeps. Montgomery visited Irvine only once after leaving as a youth, in 1841, when he was made a Freeman. There is a statue of him in Sheffield.

High Street at the Cross

This early photograph of the High Street looks north-west towards the Cross. The ornate three-storey building on the left, with the arched windows on the ground floor, is a branch of the Royal Bank of Scotland. The building was erected in 1858 to plans by Peddie & Kinnear of Edinburgh. It was built on the site of some old shops, the original branch of the bank being located through a lane to the rear. To the left of the bank, in the double-storey building of which just part is visible, was the office of Gilmour & Christie, latterly Taylor & Henderson, estate agents. The light-coloured building to the right of the bank was in the 1960s a bicycle shop, then Stagecoach bus company's offices. Next again were the premises of James Reid, the baker, which became the Hosiery Shop, and recently Meridian Room beauty salon. In the same block was S. B. Yuille's shop, one of many stationers in the town in 1900. The smaller light-coloured building, with a nepus gable at eaves level, was at one time MacCall's drapery. The shops beyond contained Walker's newsagents, book and record shop, then John S. Begg's stationery shop. Some of these were demolished and replaced with new shops in 1982-86.

Beyond the Cross, the light-coloured three-storey building is the King's Arms, one of the oldest inns in Irvine. Many major events in the history of the town took place here, and among its famous visitors were William IV, Prince Napoleon of France (1839), and Major James Burns and Colonel William Burns, sons of Robert Burns (1844). On the extreme right of the picture is the Cross Well. The building with its gable facing the street, and the external stairway, was at the time of Robert Burns' time in Irvine (1781) occupied by James Templeton. He was a bookseller, and the poet became friendly with him. Indeed, when Burns was collecting subscribers for his Kilmarnock Edition of poems, Templeton not only subscribed, but collected the money from other subscribers in the town and passed it on to Burns.

Fullarton Street

This photograph was taken from the roof of the parish church, looking across the river to what is the community of Fullarton. To the left, the row of houses perpendicular to the river (Fullarton Terrace) was attached to the laundry, just visible, with the line of skylight windows. Before being a laundry, this was M. Paterson & Co.'s, then Andrew Watt's ropeworks, the four-hundred-yard-long rope walk extending along the foot of the gardens behind the street. In the 1850s there was also a chemical works here. At the end of the lane was Lyle's Free School, where 138 pupils were taught. The school existed from 1839 until after 1870. Fullarton Street extends to the right, as far as Fullarton Place and the Irvine Bridge. This street was often referred to locally as the Soor Milk Raw, from the fact that the facades were white-washed. Immediately behind is Loudoun Street Primary. This had its foundation as Fullarton Free Church School, but it was taken over by the school board in 1872. At the left-hand end of the bridge, facing the Fullarton Hotel, was Victoria Buildings, a block of five shops. To the right of the Wilson Church steeple are the tenement blocks of Church Street, facing Fullarton Parish Church. To the left of the steeple can be seen the tenements of Friars' Croft. Between the two it is possible to make out Cochrane Street School, erected in 1905. Not in the picture, being located further along Fullarton Street to the left, was a small church and the large Greenbank Factory. This was a hosiery factory, owned by Messrs A. Cunningham Ltd. It was extended in 1928 to plans by William Campbell. On the Irvine side of the river, the double-storey building in the foreground is located in the Puddle Ford. The ford had long-gone by the time of the picture, but it was one of the original crossings of the river, meeting up with Fullarton Street through the Laundry lane. Fullarton Street was created in 1776 but was mostly demolished in 1968.

Town Centre and Hill Street

Another photograph taken from the steeple of the parish church, this one is looking across Hill Street and the Bridgegate to West Road and beyond. The dominant building in the centre of the image is the former Trinity Church. This magnificent building was erected in 1863 as a United Presbyterian Church, but took the name Trinity at the behest of its popular minister, Rev William Bruce Robertson (d. 1886). The building, with its 170-feet steeple, was designed by Frederick T. Pilkington, winner of an architectural competition which had nine entries. The steeple proved to be unstable, so had to be reduced seven years later. It served as a congregation of the Trinity Church (eventually becoming a Church of Scotland congregation) until 1966, when it merged with the Wilson Fullarton church, using the latter's building, and taking the name St Paul's. In front of the Trinity Church is the double-storey Hill Cottage, at one time owned by the Ferguson family, including Hugh Ferguson Boyd (d. 1895). He was a keen horse-racer, and his six-year-old horse, 'Voluptuary', won the Grand National in 1884, ridden by Ted Wilson. The house was later occupied by Alexander Gilmour, solicitor.

The double-storey house at the top of Hill Street, but facing onto Kirkgate, was Kirkgatehead House, originally the Free Church Manse. Here lived Anne Ross Cousin (1824-1906), who wrote many hymns. For a number of years the house was the property of George Paulin (1812-1898), Rector of Irvine Royal Academy. Paulin was much respected in the town, and he wrote numerous poems, collections of these including *Hymns and Poems*, and *Hallowed Ground and Other Poems*, the latter being published in 1876. He retired in 1877 but the school board could not offer him a pension. A public collection raised £1,000 instead, regarded at the time as 'probably the largest sum ever presented to any teacher in Scotland'. A bust of him was presented to Irvine Royal Academy in 1912 by his son, Sir David Paulin (1847-1930), born in Irvine, and regarded as being the first man ever to be knighted for his services to the insurance industry.

Bank Street

Bank Street was named after the branch of the Ayr Bank which was located to the left of the photographer. The branch opened in 1786 and was demolished in 1828, when Bank Street was created, though originally only as far as East Road. At a later date the site was occupied by the Union Bank of Scotland, which remained until 1858. Later on, New Road was laid out, extending the street to join with the end of Cotton Street. This became the main route to the north; New Road being renamed as part of Bank Street. This old picture dates from the early twentieth century. On the right, the tall building is the masonic temple, erected in 1904. On the ground floor are five shop premises. At the time the picture was taken, the shop to the right of the arched doorway was a butcher. Next door was the Glaswegian George Green's Picturedrome, a popular cinema that opened in 1912 under the management of Sam Stott. The main hall could seat an audience of 400, plus 300 in the stalls and 220 in the balcony – a total of 920. In November 1929 this was the first cinema in Irvine to introduce 'talkies', a new sound system for this having been installed. In 1965 it was renamed the Rex Cinema. In 1976 the cinema was restored and reopened as the George, the original George having burned down in 1969. Irvine at one time had six cinemas – the Empire (renamed the Regal), George, Kyle, Palace, and films were often shown at the Tivoli Theatre in West Road. Beyond Green's picture house are a line of dwellings, the first being the premises of J. F. Longmuir, grain merchants, with its first-floor bay window and ornate overdoor canopies. Beyond are the offices of Murray, Gillies & Wilson, solicitors, the firm being established in the High Street in 1906. Previously, this was occupied by Boyd & Wilson's solicitors office. This part of Bank Street terminates in a large building over three storeys, built as a hosiery factory in 1924 and known as the Ontario Buildings.

Harbourside

This picture was taken looking east along Harbour Street from the end of the Upper Wharf, near to the Ship Inn. This is claimed to be the oldest public house in Irvine, opened in 1750 by Charles Hamilton, provost of Irvine, and licensed in 1754. In the mid-nineteenth century this street was known as The Shore. On the right-hand side is the end of John Street, a short roadway that linked the harbourside with Peter Street, later renamed Gottries Road. At the end of John Street were two public houses. That on the west side of the opening, and just visible on the right of the picture, was the Garnock Inn. At the turn of the twentieth century this was owned by William Nisbet, who also owned the tenement block behind in John Street. On the east side of the road, with the corner doorway, was the Portland Arms Inn. This was later converted into a fish and chip shop, operated by Carl Guazelli, known as La Marina Café. The building was later demolished and a modern replica was built on site, now a house. The light-coloured shop between the boat and the shelter was at one time the harbour post office (1920s), but before this it was located next door to the Garnock Inn. The more modern blocks of houses before the gable were built around 1900 on what had been a timber yard. The houses are known as Scotnish Terrace, nearest the photographer, Annickbank and St Inans. Each block contains four flats. In the line of buildings beyond was the Victoria Hotel, later renamed the Harbour Lights. The slip in the centre of the picture occupies the site of the old Ballast Dock. In the left distance can be seen the timber yards, of which Irvine had a number at the turn of the twentieth century. One of the longer-lasting was that of Matthew Wright & Nephew, which was established here early in the nineteenth century. Their phone number was originally Irvine 2. The firm was later taken over but remained in operation until around 2003.

A Look Back at IRVINE ~ page 31

Parish and Trinity Church

This photograph was taken from near Merryvale farm, which was located where the present Merryvale Road takes a sharp left, just before the Golffields footbridge. The farm only extended to 3½ acres and was at one time also a bleachfield. Much of the field in the foreground was never built-up, and remains open grassland to this day. To the right can be seen the Town House, and the prominent building is the parish church. This building, one of the finest in the town, was erected in 1771-74 at a cost of £2,473 12s 9¾d to plans by David Muir of Irvine. It replaced the ancient church of St Mary, which was on the same site. In 1721 the steeple of this old church was found to be unsafe, and thus was demolished, the stone used to line a well in Bridgegate. A separate Lady Chapel is said to have existed at the south-east of the cemetery extension. When first built, the new parish church had seating for 1,800 worshippers and there was no steeple - it was not added until 1778. The council visited Dundee to inspect a new church steeple there, and decided to go ahead with a steeple at Irvine, regarded as being the first to be built in Ayrshire. The bell was the gift of the 12th Earl of Eglinton in 1797. The original roof the church proved to be too heavy for the walls, so in 1830 it was decided to remove it, raise the height of the walls by six feet, add iron columns to support the balconies, and construct a new roof. To the left of the church, the long roof is of the church hall. This was erected in Kirkgatehead in 1894-96, through the exertions of the parish minister, Rev Henry Ranken. It occupies the site of the old burgh school and was designed by the Irvine architect, John Armour Sen. (c.1842-1915). It cost around £1,300. To the left is the Trinity Church, referred to elsewhere. At the far left of the picture the building is part of Fullarton Terrace.

Low Green

A peaceful view across the River Irvine, this postcard depicts the Low Green, originally simply called The Green. To the left is the footbridge that was erected in 1886 to link the foot of Castle Street with Waterside. Just to the right of the bridge is the Slaughter House of 1843. This replaced an earlier facility, located in a former tannery, which was established in 1812 and was located at the end of West Road, next to Castle Street. In 1831 there was an outbreak of cholera across the country and the council decided to try to prevent it coming to Irvine. A sewer was constructed to remove stagnant and foul water, emptying it into the river. The slaughter house was described at the time as being in a 'filthy and abominable state', hence plans for the new facility of 1843. In 1930 there were plans for a newer slaughterhouse, but these did not materialise, and the old building was demolished in 1953. To the right of the picture is the Irvine Royal Academy building of 1901. To its left was The Butts, the location of the archery competitions which were held in the town. Beyond the Academy was the site of Irvine gallows. This was where murderers and others were executed, and a cross of boulders in the ground marks the spot. It was here that the two Covenanters, James Blackwood and John MacCall, were hanged on 31 December 1666 before burial in the kirkyard. They had taken part in the Pentland Rising. Near to the site of the gallows was the Gallows Well. The Low Green itself was used for hundreds of different events in the life of the town. The annual Cow Fair attracted scores of farmers and hundreds of cattle. Demonstrations by striking miners were held there, as were religious meetings. Football matches were held. Latterly, the green was used for leisure purposes, as can be seen by the swings and roundabouts. The putting green was opened in 1922 by Provost Walter Muir. A competition held on the day attracted 300 entries, with prizes presented by the council.

Old Tolbooth

The old Tolbooth dated from 1745, when an earlier tolbooth was rebuilt at a cost of about £450. It contained the council meeting room, at the western end, and the constabulary office at the east. The cells had walls four feet thick, their roofs being vaulted, probably much older than the rest of the building. It is known that witches and Covenanters were held here, as well as numerous miscreants from the burgh. On the exterior walls were the burgh arms and the royal arms were carved in stone higher up. Within the tolbooth tower was a clock with bell, the latter rung each evening at ten o'clock to indicate curfew time. The bell was inscribed *The Tolbooth Bell of the Burgh of Irvine 1637*. On 26 November 1740 the tolbooth was struck by lightning, causing it considerable damage, and several prisoners were severely injured. The tower was rebuilt 1818. The tolbooth was demolished in 1860-61 when the new Town House was erected in the street-line, allowing the High street to be opened up more, improving traffic flow. The tower of the Town House is seen in the centre of the image.

In front of the Tolbooth in this old photograph can be seen the Tron weighing machine. This was used on market days to check that goods being sold were of the requisite weight. It survived for a time after the Tolbooth was demolished, and was removed in 1866.

On the left are two inns – the Whip Inn, with the sign and arms over the door, and the Wheatsheaf Inn two doors down. The Wheatsheaf was where Robert Burns spent some time when he lived in Irvine in 1781. The Lodge Irvine St Andrews freemasons met here, and Burns attended some of their meetings. It was here in 1854 that Robert Bruce Mantell was born, son of the owners. He became an actor, making his professional debut on the stage at Rochdale, Lancashire. He emigrated to the United States in 1878, setting up his own company to perform classic and romantic plays. He died in 1928.

High Street Looking East

This early picture shows the High Street looking in a south-easterly direction. On the immediate left-hand side is part of the Eglinton Arms Hotel, a coaching inn that has served the residents and travellers for many years. It is thought that it was established in 1719, at the time a single-storey building. It was extended upwards in the early nineteenth century. Many functions and banquets were held here over the centuries. After the annual two-day examination of the Royal Academy, the magistrates, ministers and others dined here. When the telephone was introduced to Irvine in 1886 the hotel had the distinction of having telephone number 1. In 2010 the hotel was renamed The Carrick, operating as a pub and restaurant. Next door, the light-coloured three-storey building was occupied by A. T. Duncan, chemist. For many years it was George Watson's chemist shop.

Beyond the Bank Street junction on the left is the southern end of High Street, with the Town House to the left. To its left, with the gable facing the street, is the old Wheatsheaf Inn, which was said to date from the 1700s.

On the right of the picture is the shop operated by J. & E. McMillan, selling baby linen and other goods. Next door was the Crown Dairy, occupying premises that were previously run as a watchmaker and jewellers by Robert Crawford. At the corner with Bridgegate was J. S. Begg's bookshop and stationers.

Beyond the Bridgegate entry can be seen Greenlees' shoe shop, selling 'city styles at city prices'. Previously, the shop was run by the shoemaker, William Higgins & Co. Beyond it, the wider section of the High Street is lined by a number of fine buildings. The David Boyle (1772-1853) statue can be seen standing at the side of the street. This was erected in 1867 by public subscription, the work by the sculptor Sir John Steell. Boyle became an advocate in 1793, served as a member of parliament, and succeeded as Lord Justice General in 1841. He is noted as being the judge who sentenced the murderer Edmund Burke, of Burke and Hare infamy.

Harbour

The confluence of the rivers Garnock and Irvine has created what is a safe harbour on the Ayrshire coast, used for centuries by sailors. Only the difficulty of crossing the Irvine Bar at various tides has been an issue, and the creation of stone rubble groins has helped to keep the river to a narrow and deeper channel. The other main issue for Irvine was the fact that the harbour was in the parish of Dundonald, and thus originally beyond the control of the burgh. Irvine originally had its own simple dock at the foot of the Seagate, but the longer route required to reach the spot, and the shallowness of the water, always meant that it could never compete with the port at Fullarton. In 1677 the present harbour was established, and by 1760 Irvine was the third largest port in Scotland, with 77 vessels. In 1867 an 'Irvine Harbour Improvement Order' was passed, allowing the creation of new wharves, embankments and jetties. Nevertheless, the harbour often silted up, resulting in the harbour company requiring to operate dredgers, including the *Slaney* and then the *Irvine*. In 1906 the Tide Signal tower was erected, the unique workings having been designed by harbourmaster, Martin Boyd (1846-1918). The principal export from the harbour was coal, originally mined in the parish, but latterly brought from further inland in the county. Most of this went to Ireland. Tobacco was often imported by the Glasgow tobacco lords. Other imports over the centuries included grain, wine, butter and timber. The first real shipyard was opened in 1759 and was to be joined by others over the years, including Gilkison Thomson & Co, Irvine Shipbuilding & Engineering Company (1898-1904), Mackie & Thomson (1912-1928), and Lithgows (1928-1937). Among the ships built in the yards were the various *Baron* ships for H. Hogarth of Glasgow, and *Clan* ships for Cayzer (Clan Line, including the largest ever built in Irvine, at 7,600 tons). The last two vessels to be built at Irvine were the *Coulmore* and *Coulbeg*, launched in 1936.

Townhouse

The folk of Irvine know their town hall better as the Town House. It was erected in 1859-62 to replace the old Tolbooth which stood in the middle of the High Street. The architect was James Ingram (1799-1879), who designed many Ayrshire buildings. This one was Italianate in style, much against the wishes of the Provost, Thomas Campbell of Annfield. Accordingly, he boycotted the laying of the foundation stone, which took place in 1859, the act carried out by Bailie John Niven. The builders were Walter MacLachlan and family. By the time the building was completed, around £4,000 had been spent on it. The tower is 120 feet in height, rising centrally from the front façade, terminating with a wind vane. This comprised of a representation of a sloop, the vane taken from the old tolbooth. The town hall was opened in May 1862. Within was originally a court house and council chamber, plus meeting rooms for the Road Trustees, Collector of Customs and Irvine Presbytery. The main hall on the first-floor measures 48 feet by 27 feet, becoming a great boon for the town, and where dances, meetings, exhibitions and shows were held. Here also was the library. Portraits of local dignitaries were displayed, as was one of Provost Campbell, but this wasn't unveiled until his death in 1864. The railings in front of the town hall were removed in 1940 as part of the war effort. On 14 July 2017 the Town House was formally reopened after a period of refurbishment and the addition of the Portal Leisure Centre to its south-eastern side. The photograph was taken in the 1970s. To the right of the town hall is the timber hut used for some time by the police. The sandstone building behind it was the main police station, erected in 1860, replacing the old cells in the tolbooth. It was extended in 1892. This served the town until 2003, when a new police station was erected in Kilwinning Road. The old station was demolished and the site forms part of the Portal leisure centre.

Irvine Bridge

This photograph was taken in November 1972, looking down on Irvine Bridge. There has been some form of crossing in this vicinity for centuries, the site now occupied by the Rivergate Mall, erected in 1975-76 to plans by John K. Billingham. The bridge was closed to traffic on 10 June 1973. When the river was first bridged here is unknown, but perhaps there may have been a timber structure as early as the fourteenth century. The first stone bridge crossing the river in four arches is thought to have been constructed around 1500 – in 1578 all of Ayrshire was required to fund its repair. In 1748-53 a new bridge was built, the carriageway only being eleven feet wide, at a cost of £350. In 1826 the bridge was widened to 25 feet designed by John Herbertson. The bridge shown is the 1887 structure, being widened by the addition of cast iron brackets supporting a new pavement, resulting in a deck of 38 feet. At the left-hand side of the bridge is the Fullarton Arms Inn. On the Bridgegate side of the bridge is Dick's showroom and to its left the pagoda toilets. The white house to the right of centre is Waterside House. The low buildings to the left of it were originally Irvine Brewery. This was established in 1825 by David Gray, a local councillor, town clerk and bank agent. The buildings incorporated a malt house and brew house. In 1875 the Irvine Brewery Company was sold to John Drummond, then in 1895 to Matthew MacNaught. It was latterly taken over by Glasgow firm, A. G. Barr, famed for its 'Irn Bru'. To the right is Hamilhill cottage. The church building was originally Irvine Free Church. This building was erected in 1844-45 to plans by Black & Salmon of Glasgow. In 1900 it was renamed the Mure Parish Church. Anne Ross Cousin (1824-1906), wife of the minister, Rev William Cousin, was a noted hymn-writer, among her better-known works being 'The Sands of Time are Sinking', 'O Christ, what burdens bowed Thy head' and 'King Eternal, King Immortal'.

Fullarton Bridgend

Taken from the new high-rise flats that were erected in Fullarton Street in 1968, this photograph shows the Fullarton Bridgend. On the right is the Fullarton Arms Hotel, with the Wilson Fullarton Church behind it, with its spire still complete. The upper part of this was removed due to its unstable condition. The church was established in 1843 at the Disruption, when Rev David Wilson left the Church of Scotland with most of his congregation to establish the 'Free' Church of Fullarton. At first, the church had a building erected in 1844 in the back garden of the Fullarton Inn. In 1872 work on a new, larger building seen here was commenced on the same site, to plans by Robert Baldie, opened on 2 November 1873. In 1966, at a union with the Trinity congregation, the church was renamed St Paul's, surviving as such until 1974. The Fullarton Arms Hotel has also been known as the Fullarton Inn or Fullarton Hotel over its lifetime. In the 1850s mine host was John Wyllie, also a shareholder in the schooner *Agnes Wyllie* of Irvine. Other landlords included David Boyd, James Kyle, John Lambie and Laughland Lamont. By the 1920s the hotel had been divided into four flats, in addition to the bar and small hall. Most of the shops and houses that existed in Fullarton Place have been demolished in this picture, which was taken in November 1972. Probably the only buildings in this photograph which survive are the Fullarton Parish Church and its hall plus the distant houses in Waterside. All of the houses in Friar's Croft have gone, leaving just the line of the street striking to the left from halfway up the steeple. Friar's Croft got its name from the existence of a Carmelite friary which was located near here, and which had eight acres of land, highly cultivated with fruit bushes. The friary seems to have disappeared before the time of the Reformation in 1560. Irvine Council purchased the lands in 1750 and the feus hereabouts probably date from soon after.

Irvine Royal Academy

Irvine Royal Academy is one of few schools which contain the 'Royal' appellation. The original school was located in Kirkgatehead. In 1572, King James VI provided funds to found the King's School of Irvine. A new building was erected in 1814-16, the foundation stone laid on 22 April 1814. At the event there was a parade of two bands, freemasons, town councillors, ministers, members of the local trades, 370 pupils plus others who had subscribed to the cost. The building was designed by David Hamilton. The school was opened on 3 July 1816, at which time the old schools in the burgh were closed. At the time, it was decreed that the 10 December every year should be a holiday for the pupils in Irvine, to mark the birthday of Hugh Montgomerie, 12th Earl of Eglinton. A Royal Charter was granted in 1818 for the directorship of Irvine Royal Academy, which included the Earl of Eglinton, eleven councillors and all who subscribed £50 or more. In the mid nineteenth century, the school became more select, pupils paying fees to attend. Fees were abolished in 1927. The school was taken over by Irvine School Board in 1872. The old school became unsuitable for education purposes and in 1899 it was demolished to allow the erection of a new building. This was designed by local architect, John Armour. The new school, built of red sandstone, was opened on 27 December 1901 by the Earl of Eglinton. At the time the name Irvine Royal Academy was revived. An Annexe on Kilwinning Road, on the academy's sports field, opened in 1932. The school's primary department was closed in 1952. A new school building was planned to replace the Royal Academy, but this became Ravenspark Academy, opened in August 1969. The old buildings remained open to serve pupils from Dreghorn and Kilwinning. In August 1992, the two academies were amalgamated into Irvine Royal Academy and in June 1993 the old school and its annexe were closed. The building of 1901 was converted into offices, known as Sovereign House. The new Irvine Royal Academy was opened by Councillor Elliot Gray on 22 March 1994.

Fire in John Street

Taken in 1968, this photograph shows firemen dowsing a blaze in a tenement block in John Street, just off Harbour Street, which is seen to the back. At the end of the street was the Garnock Inn, and the tenement behind was known as Garnock Terrace. These properties were for some time owned by John Nisbet, publican, followed by William Nisbet and his trustees. The fire engine in the picture was actually based at Kilmarnock Fire Station as their third tender – the first and second tenders were standard fire engines, whereas this had a turntable ladder. The vehicle was a Commer C7, with Grade & Leigh body, and Haydon Magirus 100 feet turntable ladder. It was registered in 1960. After the fire engine had served its time, the ladder was kept and mounted onto a different fire engine. Irvine's first 'fire station' was located in the old Tolbooth, there being reference to it in 1796. There, in a downstairs chamber, the fire engine, which would probably only be a hand-pulled cart with a pumping machine and hoses, was kept. By 1852 there were three handcarts that could be pulled by horses. In 1860 a new station was established in the old school at Kirkgatehead. In 1882 fire hydrants were inserted in various locations across the town, allowing a readier supply of water. In 1922 the local volunteer fire brigade was disbanded, and the residents had to rely on fire appliances held by the Ayrshire Dockyard Company at the shipyard, or else from neighbouring communities. The Second World War brought about a change in need, and in 1940 the council purchased a new fire engine, which was kept in a building at the Low Green. In 1970 a new fire station was erected at Pennyburn, between Kilwinning and Stevenston, which was also to cover the town. In 1980 a second fire station was built near Dreghorn, the two stations covering the district.

Irvine New Town

In 1966 Irvine was selected to be one of the five New Towns to be developed across Scotland. Unlike the other towns, Irvine was to be built around an existing community, and it was the only seaside new town. As the town centre was not being developed on a greenfield site (though a site near Perceton/Girdle Toll was considered for a new town centre), the architects and planners, Hugh Wilson and Lewis Womersley, decided to make their mark on the old burgh, demolishing great swathes of the community, especially in the Fullarton part of the town, to build the Rivergate Shopping Centre, and ancillary parking. Many residents hated the destruction of the older part of the town, but the vision at the time was for a modern community. The Irvine by-pass was constructed 1975-76, and the Bailey Bridge opened in 1971. With the addition of the Marress Bridge in 1973 the original Irvine Bridge was closed on 10 June that year. Around the town housing and industrial developments were planned, initially proposed as far as Kilmarnock to create a major city, but as the years passed these were scaled back and reduced in extent. Although Kilwinning was included in the development area, that community developed slowly itself, remaining very much separate. New housing schemes at Stanecastle, Broomlands and Bourtreehill extended to the north-east, latterly to be joined with developments at Perceton and Littlestane. Large industrial estates were planned for Riverside, heading towards Drybridge, Oldhall and Newmoor, between the town and Dreghorn. Major developments included the Rivergate Shopping Centre (1975), Magnum Leisure Centre (1976), Bridgegate House (1973), Cunninghame House (1976), and work at the harbourside. The New Town was under the control of Irvine Development Corporation, the members of which are shown in this photograph, taken on the steps of the board's headquarters – Perceton House. In 1996 the New Town was wound up, the town being left to develop naturally thereafter. At the time the population was around 34,000, some way short of the 120,000 that had at one time been anticipated to have been reached by 1986.

Montgomery School

This photograph shows the winners of the North Ayrshire Cup in 1922 – Irvine Montgomery School. The boys' football team beat Dalry Academy to take the trophy. Montgomery School was erected 1905-07 by Irvine School Board at a cost of £7,500. The first headmaster was William Mitchell Jr, who had succeeded his father, William Sr., as headmaster at Loudoun Street School. His brother, George Mitchell (1867-1937), became leader of the Rhodesian Party in 1932 and served as Prime Minister of Southern Rhodesia for a few months in 1933. Loudoun Street School had its origins as Fullarton Free Church School, opened in 1844. In 1933 it and Montgomery School were merged to form Loudoun Montgomery School, the former used for younger pupils. In 1978 a new school was erected in Ayr Road to replace both schools, but retaining the Loudoun Montgomery name. Other primary schools existed in Irvine, including Bank Street Public School, erected in 1874-75 to plans by John Armour Jr. at a cost of £4,291. Originally, it was run by Irvine Burgh School Board. Its first headmaster was William Mitchell. It closed in 1982. East Road School was originally the Industrial School, established in 1814 by the burgh council to educated the poor and deprived children of the town. In 1891 it became the East Road Public School, continuing to teach children until January 1938. St Mary's Roman Catholic School was erected at Williamfield House in 1927-28 to plans by Ayrshire Education Authority, replacing an older school held within the chapel in West Road. It educated pupils of primary age, after which they attended St Michael's College (erected at Williamfield in 1921). St Mary's closed in 1984, the children moving to St Mark's (opened 1975). More recent school buildings include Glebe Primary (1974), Woodlands Primary (1998), Castlepark Primary (1970) and John Galt Primary (1960). In the new town suburbs were Fencedyke Primary (1979), Broomlands Primary and Towerlands Primary, but these three were closed in 2014 and merged to form Elderbank Primary School. Schools for pupils with additional support needs were established at Stanecastle and Haysholm.

Visit of Queen Elizabeth

This photograph depicts the Town House and the High Street on 3 July 1956, the day Queen Elizabeth visited Irvine for the first time. She was taking part on a tour of Scotland, and visited many places throughout Ayrshire before moving on to Edinburgh. In Irvine, she only stopped for eight minutes, during which time her cavalcade of limousines stopped at the Town House, the Queen alighted to be greeted by Provost George M. Donaldson. As can be seen, the street was packed with local residents desperate to get a glimpse of her majesty as she passed through the town. Since that time, the Queen has returned on 3 July 1979 to visit some local factories (Craigie Carpets Ltd. and Canadian Dominion Contact Lenses Ltd.), in addition to the town centre, Magnum Leisure Centre and the Beach Park. On both occasions she was accompanied by her husband, the Duke of Edinburgh. In 1987 she was in the vicinity to open the new extension at Beecham Pharmaceutical's factory at Drybridge. The Duke of Edinburgh officially opened the Caledonian Paper Mill on 6 July 1989. Other royal visits included Prince Charles in 1978, when he visited the Hyster fork-lift factory, and Queen Elizabeth, the Queen Mother, who passed through in 1964 on her way to Hunterston Power Station. Before the visit of the Queen, visits by royalty were scarce. Mary Queen of Scots visited on 1st and 2nd August 1563 during her tour of the west of Scotland, when she made her way from Argyll through Ayrshire to Galloway. It is unconfirmed whether she stayed at Eglinton or Seagate castles, but it is known that she was the guest of Hugh Montgomerie, 3rd Earl of Eglinton. The next visit by a reigning monarch took place in 1942 when King George VI visited the town whilst on a tour of various Ayrshire towns. William IV is thought to have visited in the 1830s.

Home Guard and Drill Hall

This photograph shows the officers of the 3rd Battalion of Ayr Home Guard outside the drill hall in October 1944. Among the Second Lieutenants, Lieutenants, Captains and Majors is Lieutenant Sir Charles MacAndrew MP (third from left in back row). The Home Guard (originally the Local Defence Volunteers) in Irvine was established in 1940 as part of a nationwide campaign to recruit older men and those in reserved occupations to form a back-up army to assist should any emergency occur in the home country. In Irvine the 'C' Company was formed, under the command of Major D. M. MacKenzie (fifth from left in second row). There were three other units in Irvine – at the dockyard, Royal Ordnance Factory and the LMS railway works. The Home Guard stood down in 1945. Irvine actually suffered some destruction at the hands of the enemy on Wednesday 7 May 1941 when some bombs were dropped over the town. One landed at the dockyard but appears to have done little damage. Other bombs landed at the north end of the town, around Heathfield. Two council houses in Winton Road were destroyed. There were four deaths as a result of the bombs. War life in Irvine was hard, and to help feed those in need, a British Restaurant was established at the Low Green. The Royal Ordnance Factory, which was established in 1917 and which was known locally as the Shell Works, increased production of TNT, before closing in 1957. *H.M.S. Fullarton* was a land-based training camp, and other training camps were established at Gailes and on Irvine Moor. The drill hall at the Parterre was erected in 1911 for the artillerymen of the Royal Scottish Fusiliers, to join that already built in East Road in 1893-4. The building was designed by James K. Hunter. In 1967 the Drill Hall was purchased by the town council and renamed the Volunteer Rooms. After the Second World War ended, the names of those killed were added to the War Memorial in the High Street, which had been erected in 1921 to designs by A. F. Balfour Paul.

Sandbank Cottage, John Street

Sandbank Cottage, located at 4 John Street, just off Harbour Street, was erected around 1868 for Robert Crawford, watchmaker in the town. His premises were located at 107 High Street. In addition to manufacturing watches and selling items of jewellery, he was responsible for the public clock located on the front of the Harbour Master's office at the end of the quayside. His business was initially sequestrated in 1869, when his 'silver levee and Geneva watches, gold, jet and plated jewellery, electro-plated goods, table cutlery, etc.' were auctioned off in Glasgow. Sandbank Cottage, however, was to be put up for public roup in the King's Arms Hotel on 1 November 1869. At the time it had a dining room, parlour, bedroom, bathroom, kitchen and scullery. Outside, in the garden, were a coachhouse, twin-stalled stable, workshop, vinery and smoking house. Originally, the cottage was divided in two, but it latterly became one home. It was sold privately on 22 October 1869, before the sale, for £303. Crawford appears to have restarted his business, operating from a shop at 59 High Street, next door to the Commercial Inn. In the early 1900s the Cowan and Gray family rented the halves of the cottage from Mrs Isabella Sinclair or Barclay, Lainshaw Street, Stewarton. In 1948 one half of Sandbank cottage was sold by Andrew Barclay to Mr and Mrs David Maitland Cowan for £250, resulting in them owning both halves, and it remained in their family until 1980. In that year it was compulsory purchased by Cunninghame District Council, as part of their proposed harbour redevelopments, and subsequently demolished. John Street was one of the shorter streets in Irvine. In addition to Sandbank Cottage, there were a few tenement buildings. Garnock Terrace was numbers 3-5 John Street, and Rowallan Terrace was number 8-12. On the opposite side of the street from Sandbank was an old limekiln and associated limeworks in the 1850s, but this had gone by the 1890s. The Harbour Forge was located at the corner with Peter Street, but newer premises were rebuilt adjoining Garnock Terrace by 1908.

East Port and High Street

This old postcard view shows the east end of the High Street, as seen from the site of the ancient East Port. This was a gateway to the town, one that could be closed to keep out unwanted raiders in times of trouble. A second, West Port, existed at the opposite end of the town, halfway along what is now Eglinton Street. The ports were removed in 1756, by which time they were regarded as being no longer of any use. At one time there was a Port Well in the street here, a public source of water for many years. The first building on the right is the Porthead Tavern. This building stands at the corner of Glasgow Vennel and was originally erected as the house of Charles Hamilton (1704-1783). He was a prominent businessman in Irvine, being a tidewaiter at the harbour, customs collector, owner of the Ship Inn, and provost on six occasions between 1758 and 1781. A wealthy individual, he was the second person in Irvine, after the Earl of Eglinton, to own an open carriage. Hamilton was acquainted with Robert Burns, who lodged nearby in the Vennel from 1781-82, and his son, John Hamilton, remained friends with the poet for longer. It was rebuilt c. 1975. The lighter building is now occupied by the Townhead Surgery.

The black-fronted building beyond was originally the Star Inn. In 1860 the local miners held a mass meeting there to complain about wages. It has since been demolished and the Central Gospel Hall occupies the site. The double-storey terrace of shops with dormer windows still survives, though the dormers have gone. This was the Temperance Hotel, run by Mrs Gardner in 1865, where no alcohol was sold. She advertised that she 'still continues to furnish select parties, and strangers visiting the locality, with accommodation. Dinners, steaks, teas, beds, &c. Charges moderate.' Here also John Campbell, Member of the Royal College of Surgeons held his surgeries. Irvine had another Temperance Hotel, located at 153 High Street, operated by Mrs Watson. This was later to become the Clydesdale Bank.

Montgomery Street

This old postcard depicts the eastern part of Montgomery Street, stretching from the Railway Station Bridge north-eastwards towards Irvine Bridge. On the left is the Railway Inn, at the time under the proprietorship of Thomas Ferguson (around 1900). It was previously owned by James Wilson and other occupiers included John Sawers, James Robertson and William Dermot. New Street stretched from here alongside the railway to Fullarton Parish Church. One of the area's older inns, it was often referred to as the 'Pop' Inn, or Railway Tavern. In the mid nineteenth century, Fullarton Post Office was located here. The single storey houses which follow, with their dormer windows, were replacements for old single-storey thatched cottages. Local bylaws pronounced that all thatched roofs had to be removed by Whitsunday 1903. Further along the same side of the street was the Argyle Inn, being run by David Moir around 1900. Next door to it was James Hunter's drapery, often referred to as the 'Glasgow Warehouse' for he obtained most of his goods there. To the right of the picture was the Winton Arms Inn. Loudon Street strikes off at an angle here, the 'Gushet House' being the single-storey building in the angle, occupied by a sweet-shop. Montgomery Street had dozens of small shops, being one of Irvine's main shopping areas at one time. Among those that existed on the east side of the railway were drapers, butchers and baker's shops owned by the MacKelvie family. They also owned the Fullarton Laundry. There were a surprising number of bakeries in the street, in addition to fleshers, shoemakers, tailors, chemists and grocers. Also in this street, at number 8, was the registered office of Irvine and Fullarton Co-operative Society Ltd. The society was founded in 1873 and had a number of shops across the town, in particular at Bridgegate and High Street. The Co-operative Hall in Montgomery Street was used for hundreds of public meetings and events. In 1880 there were 110 members. The bulk of the buildings in Montgomery Street were demolished to allow the construction of the Rivergate Shopping Centre.

Cochrane Street

Cochrane Street was initially laid out in the second half of the nineteenth century striking north from Montgomery Street. Originally, it was a cul-de-sac, the street terminating where it met the football ground. However, the field was later built over and the street was extended to Alma Place (a continuation of Church Street on the west side of the railway. In 1905 Montgomery School was erected at the north end of the street. The picture shows the terrace of houses which backed onto the railway as they were in August 1964. Most of the residents of Cochrane Street appear to have been labourers and tradesmen, plus their families. In addition to terraces of houses, Cochrane Street was also the location of a police station. This was located on the west side of the street. Across the road from the police station was a small foundry, operated by David Flanagan Ltd. This business was established in 1925 as brass founders and engineers. At the southern end of the street, on 29 October 1936 a Mrs Armstrong was in her garden hanging out her washing when the ground gave way. Luckily, she was holding the washing line at the time, or else she would have fallen into a fourteen feet deep well, which had four feet of water within it. The old well, which is shown on the 1856 Ordnance Survey map, had been covered over with timber and earth, and the timbers had rotted. At the time, the presence of the well had long been forgotten. Another resident of Cochrane Street was Joseph Downs, an amateur antiquarian. He found numerous old coins in the harbour, as well as stone age implements in the Shewalton sandhills. Some of the artefacts were presented to museums. To the north of Church Street, the roadway was originally known as Boyle Street, after Lord Boyle, but sometime in the 1900s it was renamed as part of Cochrane Street. It was in this part of the street that the Irvine Trades Hotel was located, as well as the Scottish Knitting Mills Ltd, textiles factory.

Commerce

Irvine has always been one of the main centres of commerce for the north end of the county. The presence of the harbour, railways and roads made it readily accessible, allowing people to get to the markets and shops easily. Travellers were well supplied with the numerous inns and taverns in the town, indeed, at one time it was reckoned that there were 65 public houses in the town, in the county second only to Kilwinning for density. The image to the left is of the Winton Arms Inn, which was located at the corner of Montgomery Street and the station approach. Never a very large inn, the proximity of the railway provided a ready flow of imbibers. It gained its name from the Earl of Eglinton's secondary title, Earl of Winton, the coat of arms of which were located over the door. At the time the picture was taken it was run by William Convill (he also owned the Anchor Tavern and bought the Winton Inn in 1898 for £5,000). Earlier proprietors included Henry Brown, and before that James Wilson. The picture to the right shows the shop of G. B. Cree, 'watch and clockmaker, jeweller and optician'. This was located at 21 Montgomery Street, though also appears to have had premises, perhaps not simultaneously, at 37/41 Montgomery Street. George Cree bought the watchmaking business of Daniel Porteous in November 1894. At the time he lived at 38 Loudoun Street, having moved from Helensburgh. It is probable that he was the son of John Aitcheson Cree, pawnbroker in Irvine. In an 1898 directory, Cree advertised that he 'has always on hand a fine selection of watches, clocks, jewellery, electro-plate and fancy goods of the best quality and at moderate prices. G. B. C. having a long experience both here and in Glasgow and Helensburgh, customers may rely on all kinds of repairs having his personal attention.' Cree wasn't alone in selling jewellery and watches at the time – his competitors included James Gilchrist (established in 1835 with premises at 9 Bridgegate), Robert Crawford and Nathan Watson (both High Street).

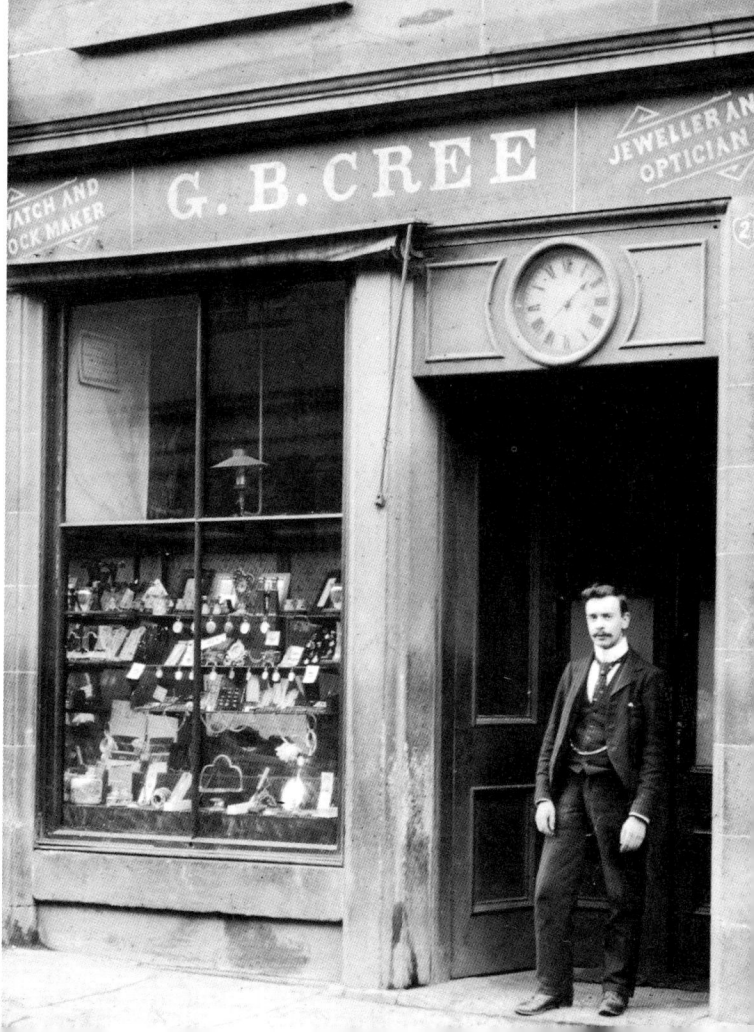

Lifeboat Station

With a busy harbour, the sailors were keen to establish some form of life-saving station. As early as 1833 a lifeboat of sorts was based in the harbour, used to assist when vessels were in trouble. In 1861 the *Pringle Kidd* was donated to the station, a self-righting vessel, thirty feet in length. The lifeboat house was erected in 1874 following considerable donations from William Somerville, whose father-in-law was a native of the town. At the same time, he donated a new lifeboat, named after his mother, the *Isabella Frew*. The *Busbie* served the town from 1887-1898, named after the estate of the donor, H. R. C. Wallace of Busbie and Cloncaird. In 1898 a new boat, the *Jane Anne*, was provided, built at Ardrossan. The lifeboat station was closed in 1914, due to a lack of suitable sailors, being replaced with the station at Troon. The lifeboat station building was converted to a bathing station in 1927 and was eventually demolished in 1966. The lifeboat at Irvine was involved in a good number of rescues, and various ships were attended, resulting in numerous lives being saved. Probably the most significant was the *Frey*, a Norwegian vessel which lost its mast in a storm on 29 December 1894. The whole crew was saved by the lifeboat, but as it made for Troon's South Beach it capsized. All managed to get back on board apart from one, who couldn't swim. Sixteen seamen from the ship were saved, though unfortunately Lars Magnusen was drowned. As a result, David Sinclair, coxswain for 32 years, and his crew were awarded medals for their bravery by the Norwegian government. The twelve lifeboatmen also received silver medals from the R.N.L.I. The presentation was made in the town hall by Provost William Breckeridge, the Norwegian medals presented by George Paton, Norwegian Vice-Consul at Troon. Over £400 had been raised by the public, and each crewman was awarded £25, Sinclair receiving £75. The widowed mother of Magnusen was given £15. The original barometer, installed in the lifeboat station in 1861, was discovered in 2015 and is located in the Burns Club, Wellwood, Irvine.

Robert Burns Statue

The statue of Robert Burns, which stands at the Gallows Knowes on the Town's Moor, was sculpted by J. Pittendreigh MacGillivray. It was presented by John Speirs, a native of Irvine who was a marine insurance agent in Glasgow. He retired to West Kilbride. The statue was unveiled on Saturday 18 July 1896. The statue is of bronze, measuring nine feet in height. The twelve-feet tall pedestal is of Aberdeen granite, on which are four bronze panels, three of which depict Burns leaving Highland Mary, the Cottar Returning, and Burns with the poetic Muse. Speirs was made a freeman of the burgh for his donation. The photograph shows the statue soon after it was erected, at which time it still had the iron railings around the gardens adjoining it. The connection of Burns with Irvine commenced in mid-summer 1781, when he came to the town to learn flax dressing. Initially he worked with a relative, William Peacock, but he appears to have been a rogue, and Burns left him. He then worked in a flax mill just off the High Street, near to the King's Arms Inn, but the exact spot is no longer known. The flax heckling shop where Burns worked with Peacock survives off the Glasgow Vennel, and the house where he initially lodged was at 4 Glasgow Vennel. A plaque was affixed to this house in 1926. The second workshop in the High Street was destroyed by fire. Whilst in Irvine Burns is known to have written 'Winter – a dirge' and 'Prayer under the pressure of violent anguish'. Burns became friendly with a variety of Irvine folk, including Richard Brown, a sailor, who is said to have encouraged him to have his poems printed. Burns was also friendly with Provost Charles Hamilton, who lived where the Porthead Tavern is now. The provost's son, Dr John Hamilton, became an even closer friend, and stood surety to John Wilson, printer of the Kilmarnock Edition of Burns' works. A holograph of the 1786 printer's copy of Burns poems is held in the Wellwood Burns Museum, home of Irvine Burns Club.

High Street north of the Cross

The High Street continues north of The Cross as far as the Seagate, where it become Eglinton Street. Half of this latter street was probably at one time regarded as being part of the High Street, for the North Port was half way along the street, marking the northern end of the original burgh. Although the northern part of the High Street appeared to be less important than the southern half, due to the latter having the Town House and Tolbooth before that, this was still an important commercial centre. On the extreme left is the edge of the King's Arms Hotel, one of the town's oldest coaching inns. When it was established isn't known, but it was sold in 1802 by Thomas Young. At that time it had a kitchen, eleven rooms, bar, cellar and a ballroom, the latter measuring 32 feet by 18 feet. In the early 1800s, King William IV stayed here, and in 1839 Prince Napoleon of France (later Napoleon III) stayed whilst attending the Eglinton Tournament. Following on is a line of shops, William Findlay first of all, then the light building being A. K. Steel jewellers for a time. Next to it was John Currie's bakery, latterly Lipton's. The three-storey building was erected on the spot where John Galt (1779-1839) was born.

He wrote dozens of novels, many of which are still in print, including *The Ayrshire Legatees* and *Annals of the Parish*. The building was demolished and replaced with a modern Bank of Scotland building. Further along the street is the Clydesdale Bank building. Next to it was the Temperance Hotel, where residents could stay overnight, but without the option of alcohol. Next door was the post office, relocated here in 1910 from the Bridgegate. A few doors along from the post office was a branch of the Union Bank of Scotland. Most of the shop fronts on the right of the picture were subsequently demolished and new facades built in line with the Eglinton Arms, widening the street by the same width as the 'Parker's' sign.

Marymass Festival

The tradition of Marymass goes back centuries, though the present format only dates from 1928, when the festival was resuscitated. In 1386, when King Robert II granted the land on which the original tolbooth was erected, he requested a rent of one silver penny, payable on the feast of the Assumption of the Blessed Virgin (Mary). This took place on 15 August. In 1572 the Earl of Eglinton was given the right of 'having the use and rycht of the keeping of the heid fair of the said burgh halding yeirlie at our first terme day quilk is the xv day of August past memour of man'. This right was removed in 1747 when heritable jurisdictions were abolished across Scotland. He was given £7,800 in compensation. Following the change in the calendar in 1753, the town council took out an advertisement in the *Glasgow Journal* in which they announced, 'By order of the Magistrates and Town Council of Irvine, the annual fair of the said burgh, commonly called Marymass Fair, which formerly began on the first Tuesday of August, and continued all that week, is this year to be kept the third Monday of August, new style, and yearly in all time coming, upon that day, and to continue the following days of the week.' In 1670 the Irvine Carters' Society was founded, and quickly established an annual horse-race which was held at Marymass. The 'Draff' race was held for competing draught horses, and these originally took place on the old race course at Bogside. When the new Bogside Race Course was established in 1808, a Cadgers' Race Course was laid out, though this may have already existed, for in 1793 the council contributed £1 10s to John Watt for expenses in making a new course. The more modern version of Marymass associates the fair with the visit of Mary, Queen of Scots, in 1563. Thus, the festival has a Marymass Queen, who is supported by her 'Four Marys', similar to the monarch. The picture shows the Marymass Queen of 1954, Anne Dale, as she makes her way along Montgomery Street.

Seagate Castle

The oldest part of Seagate Castle is at the west end, which may be the remains of Irvine Castle. From its style, this tower may date from the fourteenth century. In 1546, on the death of his father, the castle became the property of Hugh Montgomerie, 3rd Earl of Eglinton. A new 'palace' block was added. Externally the new block was built for show, with ornamental stonework, for by now the building no longer need to be defensible. Hugh Montgomerie left his mark at numerous locations on the castle. In the vaulted entrance pend, the roof-bosses bear his arms, and that of Lady Agnes, as well as their initials. The castle was used by Lord Eglinton as his town house. By the eighteenth century the Eglinton family's sphere of influence had spread much further, and a town house in Edinburgh was now needed, and Eglinton Castle became the family's country retreat. Seagate Castle was no longer required. It is thought to have been abandoned around 1746, and it is said that its roof timbers were used in the building of a church at Ardrossan. The castle fell into ruins after the roof was removed. Bishop Pococke, who visited Irvine in 1760, described the building as 'ruinous'. In the latter half of the eighteenth century the castle became associated with the 'free trade' and the vaults were often used to hide booty brought ashore. In 1810, with the castle becoming something of a problem in the town, and people stealing quantities of stone from the building, Hugh Montgomerie, 12th Earl of Eglinton, carried out a few repairs to the structure, and had most of the windows and doors that survived blocked up. In 1839 a major storm erupted over Ayrshire. The winds managed to blow over part of the remaining walls. Archibald Montgomerie, 13th Earl of Eglinton, had another attempt at saving the ruins in 1883, clearing debris. The Montgomeries sold the castle to Mrs Walker of Castlepark. She planned to have the castle preserved as an ancient monument. In 1945 she passed the castle into the ownership of the town.

Acknowledgments

I would like to thank a variety of people who have kindly supplied pictures and snippets of information that have been used in this book. They include Jean Bissett, Wendy Brown, the late Anne Cowan, Alison Young, and staff at North Ayrshire Libraries. The other pictures are part of the author's own collection of images, gathered over a period of time. I would also like to thank the many people who have supplied information to me over the years, not necessarily for this book. Often these notes are filed away, to be used at some time in the future.

In memory of
David Maitland Cowan, 22 July 1932 – 10 April 2017
and his wife
Anne Woodside Dale, 16 April 1939 - 26 July 2018